BAROQUE & FOLK

TUNES FOR THE RECORDER

AN UNUSUAL COLLECTION OF MUSIC ARRANGED FOR THE RECORDER, CONTAINING OVER FIFTY PIECES FROM OVER 300 YEARS OF MUSIC

T0087150

Published by
Hal Leonard

Exclusive distributors:

Hal Leonard
7777 West Bluemound Road,
Milwaukee, WI 53213
Email: info@halleonard.com

Hal Leonard Europe Limited
42 Wigmore Street Maryleborne,
London, WIU 2 RN
Email: info@halleonardeurope.com

Hal Leonard Australia Pty. Ltd.
4 Lentara Court Cheltenham,
Victoria, 9132 Australia
Email: info@halleonard.com.au

This book © Copyright 1996 by Hal Leonard

Contents

Introduction

by Ralph Wm. Zeitlin

For many years, a popular misconception existed that the recorder was originally the predecessor of our modern flute. In recent times however, it has been discovered that the two instruments developed concurrently, both the product of man's continual search for new ways to create musical sounds.

I very often encounter people who compare the trumpet to the cornetto (a Renaissance woodwind instrument based on the concept of a brass instrument), the viola da gamba to the 'cello, the piano to the harpsichord and the flute to the recorder, using the comparison as an example of the "improvements" man has made over older instruments. The fact is that the more modern concepts of musical compositions have demanded changes and inventions both stylistic and technological, to meet the requirements of expanding creativity. To compare one instrument to the other in terms of "improvements" on its older counterpart would be like saying that the quality of an adult is superior to that of a child. Can one truly compare the developed golden timbre of a mature female voice to the ethereal simplicity of a boy soprano? Likewise, though our modern trumpet renders the cornetto for example, unnecessary, the unique tonal qualities of the cornetto cannot be duplicated exactly in music which expressly calls for this instrument.

If, at times, the recorder suffers from lack of respect, the fault lies with the player and not the instrument. Fortunately, there are more and more recorder virtuosi who are aptly demonstrating this instrument's beauty and full capabilities. I am more rarely meeting people who tell me, after hearing some very impressive recorder piece, "I didn't know that could be done on the recorder!" The truth of it is that it cannot be done on any instrument without the proper attitude and approach to practicing. It is surprising to find people who can adequately play the piano or the violin after three or four years but seem to make far less progress on the recorder in the same time. Perhaps the one hundred fifty years of the recorder's "dark ages" have destroyed the legacy of instruction, including the philosophy and approach to performing, that the players of modern day instruments enjoy. Most recorder players I meet have developed a defeatist attitude after the struggle of their first attempts. After several so-called failures, the motivation is lost and the players resort to the "Easy Dances" they are familiar with.

What remedy is there, then, to overcome this attitude? First of all, we are so "result-conscious" that we have forgotten the idea of development. The archer doesn't give up after a few misses. He continues his practice without counting the number of his attempts with the understanding that he is developing his aim.

Applying this directly to the recorder, there is nothing in this book that cannot be worked out satisfactorily by any player who is familiar enough with the notes on his instrument and has a sufficient understanding of rhythm.

The selections contained in this book offer the player a sizeable scope of musical moods from lively, catchy pieces that are fun to rip through to those that are just beautifully melodic. While there may be a number of selections a player is not yet familiar with, there are probably many he has heard but never played, such as melodies from famous piano or string works of Haydn, Mozart, Bach and a great variety of others.

I have often been asked how one justifies playing Mendelssohn, Brahms, or Borodin—not to mention Scott Joplin—on the recorder. Well, first of all, any piece of music beautifully played speaks for itself regardless of the instrument. But even more to the point, how often have recorder players heard pieces for flute, violin, oboe or even voice, such as Schubert Lieder, and wished that they could play them on the recorder? Though purists might object to using any instrument but the one which the composer originally called for, there is a great joy in being able to participate in the creation of beauty whether we whistle, hum, or plunk it out with one finger at the piano. Must we learn the violin or flute in order to enjoy playing a melody from an orchestral work, just to preserve the "purity"? As a performer I have many times in basically Baroque solo recorder recitals, included pieces of Schubert, Scott Joplin, the Beatles, Arabic folk melodies and even familiar movie cartoon themes such as *Looney Tunes* or *Popeye, the Sailor Man.* As musically selective as these audiences were, they never failed to enjoy the spirit of these pieces.

Let us say then that this book contains several centuries of true musical spirit, and hours of musical enjoyment. It gathers together melodies originally written for violin or oboe, sung by trained singers and common people alike, Baroque and rag tunes, old and new tunes. Try to maintain the spirit in each which allowed these melodies to remain vital, and experience the joy of making them come alive again.

Corrente

Girolamo Frescobaldi

Ballet Anglois

Johann Kaspar Ferdinand Fischer

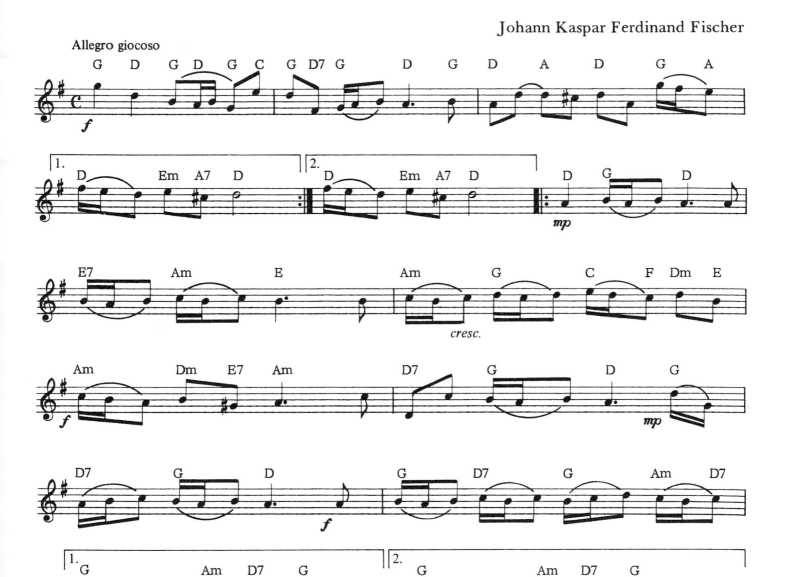

Passepied

from *Melpomene Suite*

Johann Kaspar Ferdinand Fischer

Canzoni di Danza

Vivo energico

Bernardo Pasquini

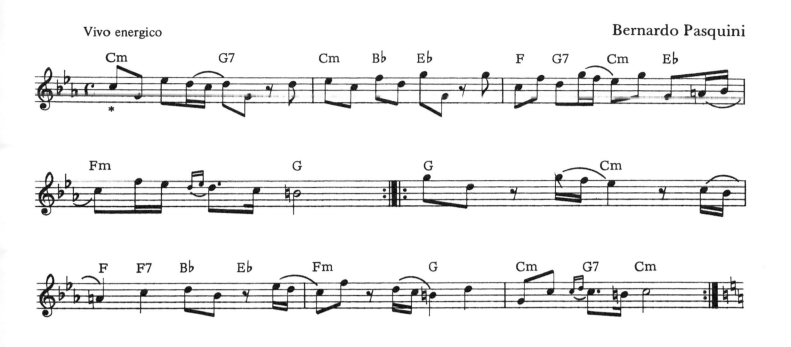

Allegro

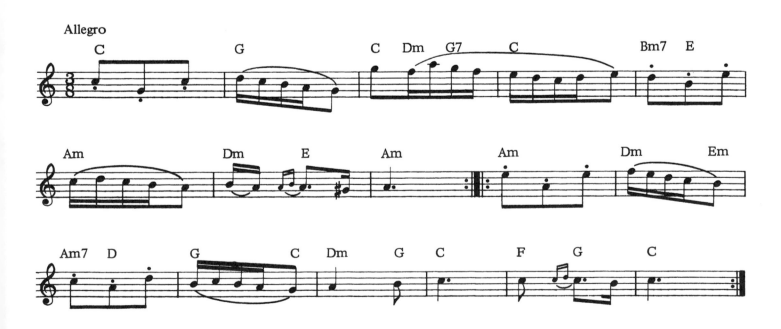

Play all eighth notes staccato

La Diane

Anglaise

Georg Friedrich Handel

Sarabande

Johann Sebastian Bach

March

Johann Sebastian Bach

Bourrée

Johann Sebastian Bach

Ayre

Antonio Vivaldi

Musette

Andantino grazioso

Johann Sebastian Bach

Trumpet Tune

Henry Purcell

Saraband

Henry Purcell

Hornpipe

Henry Purcell

Victory Dance and Festival

from *Biblical Sonata No. 1*

Johann Kuhnau

Ayre

Minuet

Georg Friedrich Handel

Passepied

Loure

Georg Philipp Telemann

Siciliana

Gottlieb Muffat

Allegro

from *Heroic Muse*

Georg Philipp Telemann

2nd time rit.

Gavotte and Bourrée

Johann Philipp Krieger

Gavotte

Christoph Willibald von Gluck

Allemande

Unknown

Andante Graziosa

Wolfgang Amadeus Mozart

Siciliana

Giovanni Battista Pergolesi

Serenade

Joseph Haydn

Andante

Christoph Willibald von Gluck

Waltz

Allegretto

Wilhelm Friedrich Ernst Bach

Allegro

Joseph Haydn

English Dance

Johann Christoph Friedrich Bach

Romance

Carl Stamitz

Der Lindenbaum

Franz Schubert

Morgengruss

Franz Schubert

Heidenroeslein

Franz Schubert

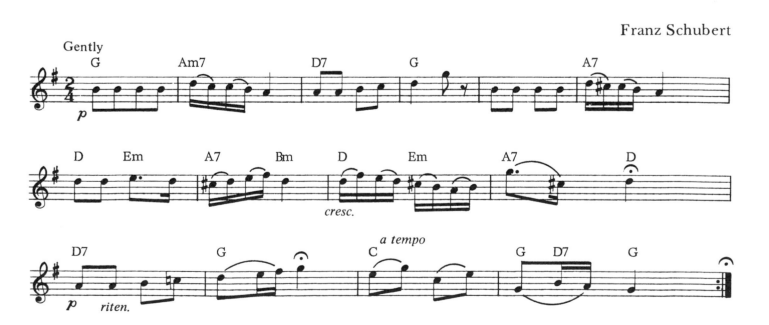

The Trout

Franz Schubert

Theme From Symphony No. 4

Felix Mendelssohn

Serenade

Franz Schubert

Poem

Andante

Zdenko Fibich

None But The Lonely Heart

Peter Ilyitch Tchaikovsky

Polovtsian Dance

from *Prince Igor*

Alexander Borodin

Serenade

Ricardo Drigo

Cradle Song

Johannes Brahms

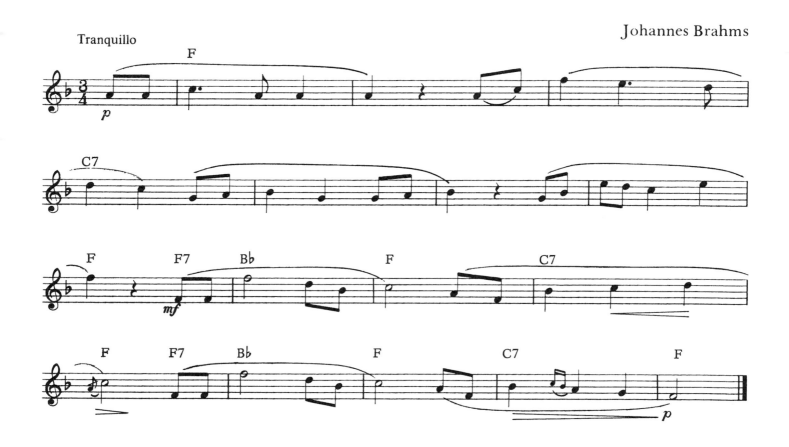

Moscow Nights

Folk Song

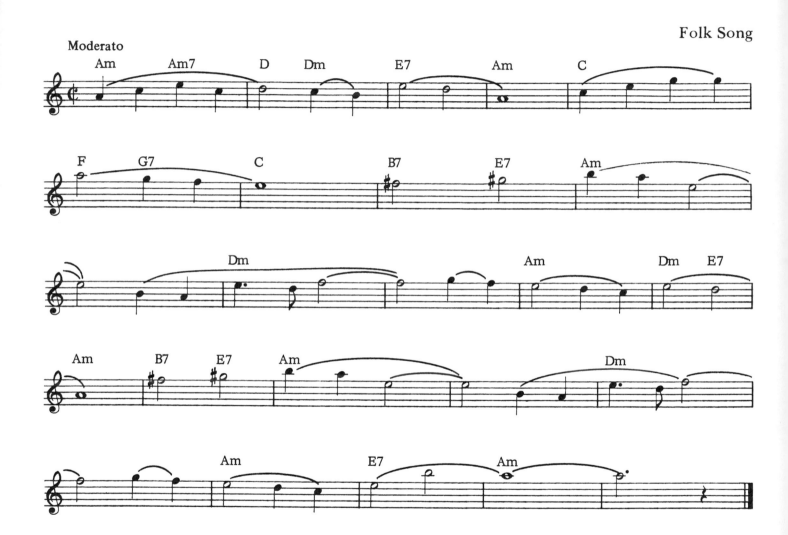

Theme from *Romeo and Juliet*

Peter Ilyitch Tchaikovsky

Theme from the Piano Concerto No. 2

Those Were The Days

Russian Song

Orientale

César Cui

Santa Lucia

Neapolitan Song

Beautiful Heaven

Cielito Lindo

C. Fernandez

Londonderry Air

Irish Melody

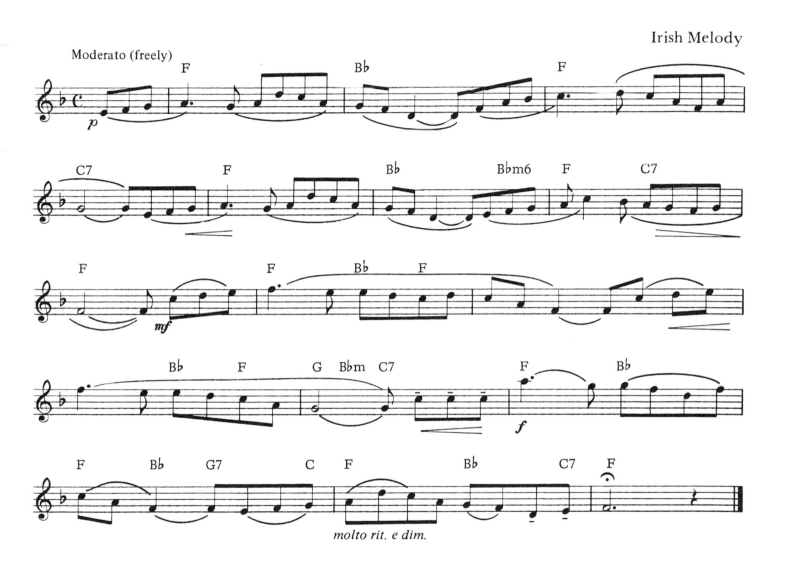

molto rit. e dim.

The Lorelei

German Folk Song

The Entertainer

Original Rags

Scott Joplin

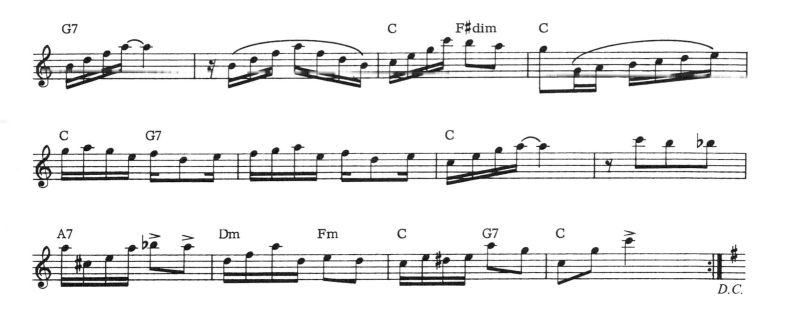

Scarborough Fair

English Folk Song

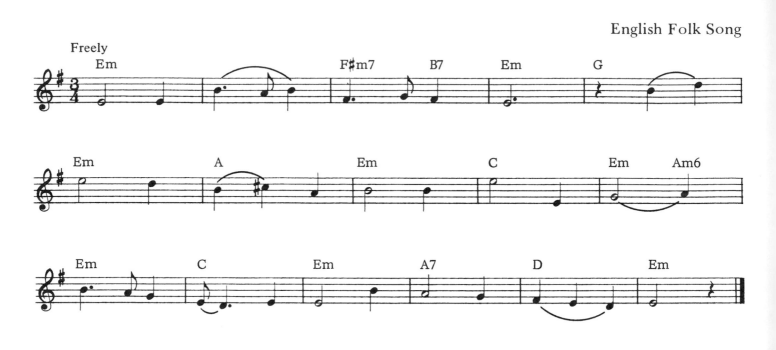

German Dance

Traditional

Amazing Grace

Traditional